HOUSE SELLERS' GUIDE

賣房122步

A Guide To Selling Your House

By

AlixFeng@gmail.com

510-770-4454 (cell)

Thank you for considering our company in the marketing of your house. The following is some information to consider when selling your property.

WHO PAYS THE REAL ESTATE COMMISSION?

It's a little-known fact that in the United State the **BUYER** pays the real estate commission. Most people mistakenly think that sellers pay the commission because they write the check to the listing and selling brokers.

However, if there were no real estate agents, prices of homes would drop by around six percent across the country. This is the value that agents add to the real estate transaction through their knowledge and experience. They also save both parties a great deal of time through their efforts and reduce liability by making sure each follows standard business practices and laws. In some parts of the country attorneys perform these service at a much higher cost.

The buyer actually pays for the brokers' valuable services because sellers increase the price of their homes by around six percent to cover the cost of the commission. Therefore, smart sellers hire the best agent available and pay the highest commission possible that will attract qualified buyers because they are actually spending the buyers' money.

WILL I BE SUCCESSFUL IN SELLING MY HOUSE?

As you may have noticed, most houses that are on the market never sell. They are simply taken off the market or relisted with another agent. Houses that do sell have the following characteristics in common:

- Seller with a definite motivation to sell.

- Seller with a definite deadline to sell.
- House that is in optimum showing condition.
- House that is priced to sell.
- Agent who knows how to target market.

MOTIVATION TO SELL

Successful sellers have a definite motivation to sell. If you just want to "See if my house will sell" or to "See how much my house will sell for" you are wasting your time.

This kind of attitude will prevent you from considering offers from serious buyers or being creative in the marketing of the house. It will also keep you from pricing your house properly.

Motivations that successful sellers have include:

- Need a larger house.
- Need a smaller house.
- Moving out of the area.
- Divorce.
- Estate planning.

DEADLINE TO SELL

Successful sellers have a definite deadline to sell. A deadline is "the soonest anything will ever get done".

Serious deadlines can include:

- Job transfer.
- Getting the kids into a new school district.
- Increasing tax deductions.
- Retirement.
- Divorce.
- Moving closer to family members
- Health reasons.

OPTIMUM SHOWING CONDITION

To bring the highest price in the shortest amount of time the house must be in perfect showing condition.   For instance, if the paint on the front door is peeling the buyer will wonder what else is wrong with the house that they can't see.

Some simple and inexpensive ways to maximize the showing condition are:

- Cut back large trees and plants.
- Paint interior walls a neutral, light color.
- Clean carpets that are soiled.
- Replace worn carpets or refinish floors (don't offer a "credit").
- Remove all throw rugs which can make rooms seem small.
- Store large pieces of furniture which make rooms looked cramped.
- Clean all windows to let more light in.
- Remove small items that can result in a cluttered appearance.
- Arrange furniture for optimum showing effect.
- Decorate the house from the buyer's perspective

When you choose me as your agent I will walk through the home with you to give you a list of specifically what you can do to optimize the showing condition of your house.

REPAIR OR GIVE A CREDIT TO THE BUYER?

In most cases, the cost of a home repair is less expensive than a potential buyer perceives the cost of the repair to be. In most cases they will double the actual cost in their minds and then deduct that from the purchase price. This is because they won't just settle for a basic paint job or carpet but will want top-of-the-line. So if you can re-carpet or repaint for $5,000 the buyer is likely to deduct $10,000-15,000 off the price if you don't do the work now. You can see how a small investment now will pay big dividends later.

PRICING THE HOUSE TO SELL

Buyers will pay what other buyers are willing to pay for houses like yours and no more. With today's technology buyers have unprecedented access to information. I will provide you with a "Competitive Market Analysis" which will show you exactly how much buyer paid in the past for comparable properties.

Do not set your price based on what you heard a neighbor got for their house. From the statistics you will find that most people do not "get their price" but to protect their egos will instead tell you they "got what they wanted". To assume they received the asking price will cause you to substantially overprice your property.

Beware of agents who try to "Buy Your Listing". In other words, agents who suggest your home is worth more than it actually is to get the listing then convince you to bring the price down later in order to get it sold. This tactic hurts you because by the time you eventually lower the price to a realistic level serious buyers have usually lost interest. If you decide to list with an agent who offers to market your house at a substantially higher price than I tell you it's worth, do yourself a favor and stick to your price.

Again, buyers will pay what the house is worth and no more. It doesn't matter how high a price you place on your house. In fact, putting an artificially high price to "test the market" can actually result in a lower than market value for your property because if you lose the most valuable marketing period (the first 30 days) the only offers you are likely to receive are low ones.

If you want the highest possible price for your house advertise it at the price that it will sell at and make sure it is in optimum showing condition.   If your price and "curb appeal" attract a lot of interest in your house it could cause a "bidding war".   If not, at least it will sell at the highest price in the shortest amount of time.

No serious agent wants to "give away" your house at a bargain price because the higher price it sell for the more commission they will earn.   However, you don't want to allow the property to sit on the market until it becomes "stale".   If this happens, buyers will wonder "What is wrong with the house" or "Why hasn't it sold yet?"   If you get any offers at this point the only offers you will get from these buyers are low offers.

If you want to get your house sold... price it right.   This way you will get the highest price and be able to move on with your life.

TARGET MARKETING

In a normal real estate market there are only two or three serious, qualified potential buyers for any house.   A good real estate professional can help you develop a marketing plan that will help you target those specific buyers.   This brings you the highest prices in the shortest amount of time.

For example, if you are selling a condominium there are specific ways to reach potential buyers for this property.   Exclusive health clubs, high-end apartment buildings and other places frequented by young professionals may be appropriate places to locate this kind of buyer.

If you own an upper-end property there is a totally different buyer for your house than a condominium.   Buyers for your property may be found at private golf clubs, tennis clubs or riding academies in your area.

The professional agent who provided you with this Guide will give you a specific plan to reach your buyers. This will maximize the price you receive and minimize your marketing time and hassles.

PUTTING A SIGN ON THE HOUSE

A "For Sale" sign lets everyone in the neighborhood know that your house is one the market. Some sellers are reluctant to let neighbors know their house is for sale. However, without a For Sale sign just imagine what neighbors think when strangers go in and out at all hours!

Some of the most likely buyers are friends or relatives of your neighbors. Haven't you ever had someone say to you, "If a house ever comes on the market in this area please let me know."

The lack of a For Sale sign can substantially reduce the ultimate selling price of your house and lengthen the marketing time necessary to sell it.

PUTTING A LOCK BOX ON THE PROPERTY

A Realtor "Lock Box" makes it easier for agents to see your house. The easier it is to view a property the likely it is to sell. Many agents will not bother to show a house that does not have a Lock Box.

The lack of a Lock Box can substantially reduce the ultimate selling price of your house and lengthen the marketing time necessary to sell it.

HELPING YOUR HOUSE TO LOOK ITS BEST

You will get the most money for your house if it shows well both outside and inside. This is known as "staging" and is a real art.   After listing your house your agent will give you a detailed list of exactly how to make it look its best but here are some basic ideas:

Outside the house:

> Paint the outside, if the paint is faded or worn.
> Trim trees and bushes back.
> Mow the lawn.
> Keep plants, lawn and bushes watered.
> Sweep walks and patios of debris.
> Wash windows and skylights.

Inside the house:

> Remove large pieces of furniture.
> Paint dark walls a light, neutral color.
> Add small plants to add color.
> Rearrange furniture to make rooms seem larger.
> Put away children's toys.
> Steam clean dirty carpets.
> Replace worn carpets.

Just a word of caution here...   Many sellers don't want to fix-up or replace items in the house and instead, offer a credit to the buyer.   The problem is that buyers will assume that things cost more to fix or replace than they actually do.   For instance, if you offer a $1,500 credit for new carpet the buyer will find a price for the very best carpet and padding available so instead of accepting your credit they will deduct $5,000 from the value of your house.   Consider installing an inexpensive, neutral color carpet and save yourself $3,500!

Be sure to put away small items and collectibles. Anything that a child could pick up and put into their pockets should be stored. It will also make rooms look larger if curios are put away.

IF YOU HAVE SPECIAL OR UNIQUE FEATURES OF YOUR HOME

One of the biggest benefits of home ownership is the ability to customize your home to the personal needs and wants of you and your family. While this may have cost a great deal of money potential buyers may not always value that feature in the same way – which means that they may not be willing to pay for it.

While some basic home improvements can increase the value of your home, many should be looked at as features that enhanced your quality of life while you lived in the home. But, when it comes time to sell, *it's time to let it go*. You enjoyed it while you lived here but not every buyer share your values and will pay for it.

SHOWING YOUR HOUSE

"Three's a crowd!" Too many people at an open house or during inspections will keep prospects from feeling free to look around your house. The only person who should be present when buyers are looking at the house are your agent and their agent (if they have one).

Keep pets out of the house during showings so that prospective buyers will feel comfortable to wander throughout the entire property. Your agent will help to minimize your pet's discomfort and maximize the house's showing potential.

Please do not discuss price, terms or any other issues with prospects. These are material facts that, by law, must be put in writing before they have any effect.

CHOOSING YOUR AGENT

Very few house sellers know how to interview a real estate agent. Some of the questions to ask your real estate professional include:

- Who specifically are the buyers for this property?
- Exactly how will you reach them?
- What makes you special as an agent?
- Specifically how can I make my house more attractive to buyers?
- What guarantee do you offer that I will be satisfied with your services?
- What is your marketing plan to get my house sold?

Remember, don't list with the agent who suggests the highest listing price for your house unless they can back up that price with comparable properties that have sold recently. If you let an agent "buy your listing" you will lose time and probably end-up selling for less than if the house had been priced properly in the first place.

If some of the agents who look at your house refuse to give you a probable selling price be very wary. They may be trying to see what price you have in mind and will simply list it for that figure whether or not the market justifies the price. Again, these agents are simply trying to "buy your listing" and will ask you to lower the price in a very short amount of time.

EXCLUSIVE MARKETING SERVICES

I do over 100 activities to get your house sold faster and at a higher price. To earn my commission some of things I do on your behalf include:

1. 訂購完整的房產文件
   Order a complete property profile of your house.

賣房 122 步

2. 看看是否準確
   Review the property profile for accuracy.

3. 做CMA估價（Competitive Market Analysis）
   Perform a complete "Competitive Market Analysis" of your house.

4. 預計買房要花多長時間
   Calculate how long it will take your property to sell.

5. 判定市場上類似房屋的影響
   Determine the effect of similar properties on the market.

6. 幫助構建營銷策略
   Help develop a pricing strategy for your property.

7. 預計售後所得
   Compute an estimation of your proceeds from the sale.

8. 向賣主提供如何準備賣房的資訊
   Provide you with information on how to prepare your property for sale.

9. 從買方角度查看賣主的房屋
   Tour your property from the "Buyer's Standpoint".

10. 做一個完整的裝飾方案
    Conduct a complete "staging" analysis of your house.

11. 提供如何最佳裝飾的書面指標
    Provide written instructors on how to stage your house for maximum effect.

12. 品評室內最佳賣點
    Review the interior of the house to maximize attractiveness.

13. 幫助賣主找到大家具的存儲點

    Assist you in locating suitable storage for large pieces of furniture.

14. 品評室外最佳賣點以便靚麗裝飾

    Review the exterior of the house to maximize "curb appeal".

15. 幫助賣主裝修室外盡量吸引人

    Assist you in making the exterior as attractive as possible.

16. 攝影以便上市

    Take photographs of your property for use in marketing materials.

17. 製作"剛上市"明信片

    Develop "Just Listed" postcards.

18. 上網推廣您的房屋

    Place your property for sale on the Internet.

19. 解釋賣主回租(seller carryback)的好處

    Explain the advantages seller carryback financing.

20. 解釋賣主回租(seller carryback)的壞處

    Explain the disadvantages of seller carryback financing.

21. 查看任何阻礙賣房的因素

    Review the status of any encumbrances against the property.

22. 評估通行權的影響

    Review the significance of any easements affecting the property.

23. 仔細做房屋目視檢查(AVID)

    Conduct a thorough and diligent visual inspection of the property.

24. 查看所有阻礙賣房的欠稅狀況

    Review the state of any property tax liens against the property.

25. 取得房屋相關的建築圖紙及許可

    Obtain architectural drawings and permits relative to the property.

26. 協助確定房屋面積大小（呎）

    Assist in determining the square footage of the house.

27. 為上市寫一篇吸引人的房屋描述

    Develop an attractive descriptive of the house for marketing.

28. 將房屋描述放到房源展示系統MLS

    Place house description into the Multiple Listing Service.

29. 解釋地產經紀人的義務與責任

    Explain real estate Agency duties and liabilities.

30. 查看買方要求的洪水揭示文本

    Review required flood disclosures, as required.

31. 查看買方要求的地震揭示文本

    Review required seismic disclosures, as required.

32. 查看買方要求的額外的地產附加稅揭示文本(Mello Roos)

    Review required Mello Roos disclosures, as required.

33. 查看自然災害揭示文本NHD的要求

    Review the environmental Hazards Disclosures requirement.

34. 查看聯邦徵收的外國投資房地產稅

    Review the federal Foreign Investment in Real Property Tax Act.

35. 查看州府徵收的外國投資房地產稅
    Review the state Foreign Investment in Real Property Tax Act.

36. 查看煙火探測器要求規則
    Review the Smoke Detector Compliance requirement.

37. 查看游泳池安全的相關法規
    Review any swimming pool safety ordinances and laws, as appropriate.

38. 提供Statement of Identity表格請賣主填寫
    Provide seller with "Statement of Identity" for completion.

39. 與賣主一起研究CMA比較市場價格
    Review Competitive Market Analysis with seller.

40. 解釋佣金如何在買賣雙方經紀人之間分配
    Explain how commissions are split between Listing and Selling Brokers.

41. 向賣主解釋代理人賣房賺多少錢
    Explain to seller how much the agents earns on the sale of the property.

42. 給賣主展示佣金分配如何影響房屋展示多頻繁
    Show seller how commission splits affect how often a house is shown.

43. 與賣主一起研究Broker Employment合同*
    Review the Broker Employment Agreement with the seller.

44. 與賣主解釋市場保證價格
    Explain my "Marketing Guarantee" to the seller.

45. 與賣主簽訂市場保證價格
    Sign "Marketing Guarantee" with the seller.

46. 評估在房產放置密碼鎖盒的優點
    Review advantages of using a real estate lock box on the property.

47. 評估在房產放置密碼鎖盒的缺點
    Review disadvantages of using a real estate lock box on the property.

48. 評估在房產前放置地產標示牌的好處
    Review the benefits of placing a real estate sign on the property.

49. 安排房產的蟲害控制檢查
    Arrange for pest control inspection of the property.

50. 安排房產的工程承包商檢查
    Arrange for contractor's inspection on the property.

51. 安排房產的屋頂檢查報告
    Arrange for roof report on the property.

52. 安排化糞池檢查報告（若需要）
    Arrange for septic tank inspection, as necessary.

53. 安排縣府許可檢查報告（若需要）
    Arrange for county inspection, as necessary.

54. 安排井水檢查報告（若需要）
    Arrange for well water inspection, as necessary.

55. 安排石棉分析報告（若需要）
    Arrange for asbestos analysis, as necessary.

56. 安排煙火警報器檢查報告（若需要）
    Arrange for smoke detector inspection, as necessary.

57. 安排節能檢查報告（若需要）
Arrange for energy conservation inspection, as necessary.

58. 安排土壤檢查報告（若需要）
Arrange for soils inspection, as necessary.

59. 協助賣主糾正檢查中發現的重大問題
Assist seller in correcting anything significant revealed in inspections.

60. 向賣主提供告知隱患的TDS（轉讓公開聲明）
Providing Transfer Disclosure Statement to the seller.

61. 填寫賣方代理人部分的TDS
Complete listing agent's portion of Disclosure Statement.

62. 向買家提供TDS（轉讓公開聲明）
Provide Transfer Disclosure Statement to buyers.

63. 在房產前放置專業的"出售"標示牌
Place a professional "For Sale" sign on the property, as authorized.

64. 在"出售"標示牌上放置合適的聯繫信息
Place appropriate riders on For Sale sign.

65. 在"出售"標示牌上放置簡介盒
Place brochure box on For Sale sign.

66. 保持簡介盒內一直有單張
Keep brochure box filled with flyers.

67. 獲得許可後在房產前放置密碼鎖盒
Place lock box on property, as authorized.

68. 直接聯繫對此房產合格的買家的經紀人
Directly contact agents with qualified buyers about the property.

69. 回答代理人關於房產的問題
Respond to agent questions about the property.

70. 回答買家關於房產的問題
Respond to buyer questions about the property.

71. 設計有吸引力的房產簡介彩色單張
Design attractive color flyers for the property.

72. 在室內單張盒中放置單張
Place flyers in flyer stand inside the property.

73. 訂一份當地學校的評分報告
Order an academic report on local schools.

74. 為潛在的買家準備財務選擇的分析表
Prepare sheets for potential buyers showing financing options.

75. 準備開門展售的來客登記表
Prepare an Open House Guest Register.

76. 與賣主或租客制訂開門展售時間表
Develop an Open House schedule with owner or tenants.

77. 協助屋主準備展售房產
Assist homeowner in preparation of the property for showing.

78. 若必要，打電話進行市場營銷
Conduct telephone calls to target market, as necessary.

79. 研製最可能的買家資料檔
Develop a profile of the most likely buyers for the property.

80. 若必要，更新市場營銷計劃
Update marketing program, as necessary.

81. 與賣主密切聯繫關注市場狀況
Stay in close contact with the seller about the status of the marketing.

82. 給不同媒體撰寫廣告詞
Write advertising copy for various media.

83. 在不同媒體上放廣告
Place ads in various media.

84. 印製彩色單張
Print color flyers.

85. 在室內明顯位置擺放單張架
Provide clear flyer display stand for inside the house.

86. 在空房間建議擺放合適的租用家具
For vacant properties suggest the use of appropriate rental furniture.

87. 教賣主如何取得建築許可的複印件
Show owner how to obtain copies of building permits.

88. 合適的話，訂購小區規章CC&R複印件
Order copies of Covenants, Conditions and Restrictions, as appropriate.

89. 輸入合適的資訊到房源展示系統MLS
Place appropriate information into Multiple Listing System.

90. 訂製專業的房屋照片以放入MLS
    Order professional photo of the property to be take for the MLS.

91. 合適的話，到周圍鄰居家敲門宣傳
    Conduct door-knocking campaign in neighborhood, as appropriate.

92. 給周圍鄰居發"剛剛上市"明信片
    Send Just Listed postcards to neighbors.

93. 跟進那些展示過本房的代理人
    Follow-up with agents who show the property.

94. 帶潛在的買家來看房
    Meet potential buyers to show them the property.

95. 按開門展售取得的聯絡方式跟進潛在的買家
    Follow-up with potential buyers from open house contacts.

96. 到熱鬧的地方去發現潛在的買家
    Canvass centers of influence to locate potential buyers.

97. 為當地代理安排房產導覽
    Arrange for a tour of the property by all agents in the area.

98. 製作計劃吸引代理參加"經紀人開門導覽"
    Develop a program to attract agents to "Broker's Open" tour.

99. 徵求其他代理對售價的看法
    Obtain other real estate agent's opinions of the pricing of the property.

100. 徵求其他代理對佈景裝飾的看法
    Obtain other real estate agent's opinions of the stage of the property.

101. 每週通過電話或電郵向賣主匯報進展狀況
Provide a weekly status report to seller by phone or Email.

102. 查看當地新聞了解鄰里動向
Review local news sources for changes in the neighborhood.

103. 若適當，放置"開門展售"廣告
Place "Open House" advertisements, as appropriate.

104. 合理放置開門展售標示牌以吸引買家
Strategically place Open House signs to attract buyers.

105. 為潛在買家開門
Hold property open for potential buyers.

106. 為開門展售的來客提供小點心和飲料
Provide refreshments for Open House guest.

107. 一定要請每位開門展售的來客簽到
Make sure every visitor signs the Open House Guest List.

108. 與賣主討論開門展售的情況
Review results of the Open House with seller.

109. 在潛在買家下單前預先確認其購買資格
Prequalify all potential buyers before offers are made.

110. 與賣主定期查看市場規劃的進展狀況
Periodically review progress of the marketing program with seller.

111. 給帶客人展示過房屋的代理發感謝函
Send "Thank you" notes to agents who show the property.

112. 定期更新房源展示系統MLS上的信息
Periodically update MLS information.

113. 協助賣主符合公平居住法
Assist seller in complying with Fair Housing Laws.

114. 協助賣主符合公平貸款法
Assist seller in complying with Fair Lending Laws.

115. 查看所有競爭出售中的房屋
View all competing houses for sale.

116. 協調遞交購房開價單
Coordinate presentation of offer to purchase the house.

117. 若需要，撰寫還價單
Write Counter-Offers, as necessary.

118. 確認代書已開立無誤
Make sure escrow is properly opened.

119. 確認購房押金已給賣主無誤
Make sure purchase deposit is properly credited to seller.

120. 確認完成過戶時所有欠款已還清
Make sure that any encumbrances are paid off at close of escrow.

121. 確認完成過戶時賣主得到了正確的款項
Make sure seller is provided with correct amount at close of escrow.

122. 還有許多雜務，不勝枚舉
Other miscellaneous activities, too numerous to mention.

賣房 122 步

Real estate business expenses typically include:

> Automobile expenses (repairs, service, tires, etc.)
>
> Auto insurance
>
> Gasoline
>
> Real estate board dues
>
> MLS fees
>
> Advertising
>
> Agent tour food
>
> Sign expenses
>
> Lock box
>
> Purchasing forms
>
> Equipment (computer, calculator, etc.)
>
> Computer on-line services
>
> Professional liability insurance
>
> Repairs
>
> Income taxes on real estate income
>
> Postage
>
> Copying
>
> Business entertainment
>
> Referral fees to other agents
>
> Cellular telephone
>
> Business telephone

Of the 1.0% left to pay taxes more than half goes to taxes (35.0% federal + 10.0% state (where applicable) + 15.3% self-employment tax) leaving most agents with less than 0.5% of the sales price of a house to pay personal living expenses such as food, clothing, housing and education for children.

ESTIMATED NET PROCEEDS FROM SALE

The most important thing you want to know from your agent is not how much the house will sell for but how much you will have after paying all expenses. Your agent will assist you in completing the Seller's Estimated Proceeds form.

INSPECTIONS FOR YOUR HOUSE

You house should be professionally inspected <u>before</u> you actively place it on the market. This way you will know if any repairs will be necessary prior to close of escrow. This can save you time <u>and</u> money in the marketing of your property.

Some inspections your agent should discuss with you include:

- Contractor's inspection
- Pest Control inspection
- Roof report
- Septic inspection (if applicable)
- Well inspection (if applicable)
- Environmental Hazards report
- Earthquake report
- Soils report
- Others, as applicable

Inspecting your house first will cost you money up-front but will usually save you much more money in the long-run. For instance, if a buyer has the house inspected and finds that repairs are needed they may cancel their Purchase Agreement. Several weeks have probably passed by this time since the house was placed on the market and most interested buyers have moved on to other properties. As with the overpriced house, now it has become "stale" on the market and the only offers you will probably receive will be low ones.

Also, by discovering that work is needed on the property early it allows you the luxury of shopping for contractors and other professionals to do the work at the best price. You, the homeowner, may even be able to do some or all of the repair work yourself saving more money.

Finally, by having the property inspected and disclosing these reports before a buyer makes their offer it reduces the chance of buyers' remorse. If the buyer discovers problems after the Purchase Agreement has been signed it creates an atmosphere of mistrust between buyer and seller.

The buyer may be willing to reimburse all of some of the inspections since it benefits them in the purchase of the house. At any rate, conducting your inspections before actively marketing the property is a very worthwhile investment for a serious seller.

SHOULD YOU SELL YOUR OWN HOUSE?

Some people think they can save money by selling their house themselves. It's a little-known fact that only 12% of "For-Sale-By-Owners" are actually successful in selling their houses. Of this group, over half end-up in court following the close of escrow. The other 88% either list their properties with a real estate professional or remove it from the market after losing money and a lot of time.

Selling a house is a very complex process as you can see from the list of things an agent does to sell your property. Even attorneys who are used to contracts and legal matters usually list their properties with a real estate agent.

The commission you pay a real estate agent to sell your house is usually deductible from the proceeds (consult your financial and/or tax advisor for the exact effect on your situation). The precious time you spend on selling your own property is not deductible.

However, if you want to sell your property you should have the following characteristics to successfully sell your own house:

- Knowledge of contract law.
- Ability to negotiate with adverse parties.
- Knowledge of marketing and advertising.
- Available to show your property whenever buyers desire.
- Financial background to help buyers qualify for a loan.
- Extremely attentive to small details.

Even if you offer a commission to an agent who brings a buyer most agents won't work with a FSBO because they know they will have to do the work done by the listing agent in addition to their own. It's usually easier to find another property where a listing agent represents the seller.

Keep in mind that because you have less ability to market your property you will have less access to buyers. This can result in a lower net sales prices than if you had used the services of a real estate professional.

If you are seriously considering selling your own house be sure to ask your agent for a "For-Sale-By-Owner Guide".

DISCLOSURE

Don't hide problems or flaws in your house or they could come back to haunt you. Tell your agent all about the property - both good and bad.

The law says you must disclose everything you know about the property and the buyer then purchases it knowingly. Your agent will help you complete a "Transfer Disclosure Statement" for the buyer.

"SHORT SALES"

Throughout the history of real estate in the United States there have been periods during which the market has been extremely slow. During such times the fair market value of a house may be less than the loans owed against it. This is known as being "upside-down" in the property.

Some owners think the only way to cut their losses is to walk away from the house by giving the lender a "Deed in Lieu of Foreclosure". This can have adverse tax consequences leading to a situation known as "Phantom Income" in which you owe tax on the lender's forgiveness of your debts. It may also adversely affect your credit rating. In addition, your lender does not have to accept the Deed in Lieu. Please consult your own tax advisor and/or attorney for the exact effect on your particular situation.

The first person to contact if you find yourself upside-down in your house is a knowledgeable real estate professional who provided you with guidance. He or she can discuss the possibility of a "Short Sale" and other options. A Short Sale is where the lender takes less than they are owed thus preserving your credit rating. Please consult your own tax advisor and/or attorney for the exact effect on your particular situation.

Why would a lender take less than they are owed? There are many legitimate reasons why a lender would cooperate with a Short Sale.

1. Banks are not in the business of owning real estate.

2. A Short Sale could cost less than repossessing a property.

3. Repairs could be needed after repossession.

4. Loss of mortgage payments could compound loss.

There are other options for upside-down properties including lease-options and loan assumptions.   A buyer might be willing to pay more than a property is worth if they can purchase with little or no money down.   Also, a lender may prefer allowing your loan be assumed by a qualified buyer rather than having to go through a long an costly repossession process.   Talk to your agent about your options.

LEGAL AND INCOME TAX CONSEQUENCES

The sale of any real property can have serious legal and income tax consequences.   The 1997 Tax Act provides that for a principal residence sold after May 6, 1997 a taxpayer can exclude gain up to $250,000 if you are single or married filing a separate tax return and up to $500,000 for couples filing a joint return.

To qualify for this exclusion you must have owned your residence for at least two of the last five years before the sale.   You must have also occupied the house as your principal residence for two out of the last five years.   These two year periods do not have to be the most recent two years nor do they have to be consecutive.

It may also be possible to defer the gain on the sale of investment property under Internal Revenue Code Section 1031.   To obtain any of these benefits you must usually plan well in advance of the sale of your property.

You should contact an appropriate tax, accounting, legal or real estate professional for the exact effect on your specific situation.

BEFORE YOU LEAVE YOUR PRESENT HOUSE

You must prepare now for your move by:

1. Have your refrigerator and other appliances serviced for the trip.

2. Lock your computer hard drive before moving it.

3. Notify your current utility companies and others that you will be leaving including:

   Garbage service
   Gas company
   Electric company
   Telephone company
   Water company
   Newspaper delivery
   Charge accounts

4. Send your forwarding address to your local post office.

5. Send change of address cards to magazines, insurance companies, book clubs, friends and stores.

6. Keep all prescriptions, eyeglasses and bank accounts in your possession at the time of the move.

At your new address be sure to:

1. Notify utility companies.

2. Check stove and water heater pilot lights.

3. Notify the Department of Motor Vehicles of your new address.

4. Register your car if you move to a new state.

5. Register children in school.

6. Notify post office

HELPING CHILDREN COPE WITH A MOVE

Moving can be a very traumatic experience for children. Everything that has been familiar to them, possibly for their entire lives, will change.

Be sure to talk with your children about the move before the "For Sale" sign goes up. Explain the reasons for the move and what the new home will be like in terms they can understand.

Always explain the relocation in positive terms... as an adventure. Tell your children how they can contribute to the success of the move. If possible, have them take responsibility for packing their own possessions and relocating them to the new home.

Encourage your children to express their feelings about the move. Try to keep your attitude positive, even if the children's attitudes are negative.

Some sellers think the best time to relocate school-age children is during the summer after school has ended. This places children in unfamiliar surroundings at a time when opportunities to make friends are at a minimum. When school opens, the child will be a stranger in a new school.

賣房 122 步

Sell your house whenever it is best for you.   Your real estate agent will be able to offer suggestions to minimize the stress of a move on your family.

MARKETING GUARANTEE

Your agent guarantees his or her services.   Enclosed is a written guarantee that the agent will complete so that you can list your house with complete confidence.

FOR MORE INFORMATION

The real estate professional who provided you with this Guide stands ready, willing and able to help you reach your goals.   Please feel free to contact him or her with any question.

PRELIMINARY ESTIMATED SELLER'S PROCEEDS

ESTIMATED SELLING PRICE $ _____

LESS ENCUMBRANCES:

     First Trust Deed or Mortgage*   _____

     Second Trust Deed or Mortgage*   _____

     Other Liens or Encumbrances*   _____

LESS SELLING COSTS:

     Optional Home Protection Plan   _____

     Seller's Escrow Costs   _____

     Real Estate Brokerage Fee   _____

     Attorney Fees   _____

     Prepayment Penalty, if any   _____

     Proration of Interest on Existing Loans   _____

     Pest Control Inspection   _____

     Roof Inspection   _____

     Contractor's Inspection   _____

     Transfer Tax   _____

     Miscellaneous   _____

APPROXIMATE TOTAL COSTS & ENCUMBRANCES _____

ESTIMATED SELLER'S PROCEEDS $ _____

*Encumbrances may vary as of date of Close of Escrow

www.ingramcontent.com/pod-product-compliance
Lightning Source LLC
Chambersburg PA
CBHW071833200526
45169CB00018B/1460